SCHOLASTIC

Success With Reading Comprehension

New York • Toronto • London • Auckland • Sydney
Mexico City • New Delhi • Hong Kong • Buenos Aires

Teaching *Resources*

State Standards Correlations

To find out how this book helps you meet your state's standards, log on to **www.scholastic.com/ssw**

Written by Kathy Zaun
Cover design by Ka-Yeon Kim-Li
Interior illustrations by Elizabeth Adams
Interior design by Quack & Company

ISBN-13 978-0-545-20081-3
ISBN-10 0-545-20081-4

11 12 13   40   17 16 15 14

Introduction

Reading can be fun when high-interest stories are paired with puzzles, riddles, and fun activities. Parents and teachers alike will find this book a valuable teaching tool. The purpose of the book is to help students at the fourth grade level improve their reading comprehension skills. They will practice finding the main idea and story details, making inferences, following directions, drawing conclusions, and sequencing. The students are also challenged to develop vocabulary, understand cause and effect, distinguish between fact and opinion, and learn about story elements. Practicing and reviewing these important skills will help them become better readers. Take a look at the Table of Contents. Teaching these valuable reading skills to your fourth graders will be a rewarding experience. Remember to praise them for their efforts and successes!

Table of Contents

Mail Call

  *The **main idea** tells what a story or paragraph is mostly about.*

Read the letters Tyler wrote from camp and those he received. Write the main idea for each letter.

Dear Mom and Dad,   Saturday, June 7

   Camp is great! I have met a lot of new friends. Jimmy is from California, Eric is from Iowa, and Tony is from Missouri. We have a great time together, swimming, canoeing, hiking, and playing tricks on other campers! Every night, we sneak over to another cabin. We then try to scare the other campers either by making scary noises or by throwing things at their cabin. It's so funny to see them run out screaming! Now

   don't worry, Mom. I'm not going to get caught like I did last year.

   One thing that is different from last year is how many bugs there are! I know that scientists discover 7 to 10 thousand new kinds of insects each year, and I think they could discover even more here! I have at least 100 itchy mosquito bites and about 20 fire ant bites. Every time I go outside, horseflies chase me, too! Other than all these buggy bugs, I'm having the best time!

                                                   Love,
                                                   Tyler

Main idea _____

Dear Tyler,   Tuesday, June 10

   Are you sure you are okay? All of those bugs sound awful! Have you used all of the "Itch-Be-Gone" cream I got you? You know how your feet swell if you don't use the cream! How about the "Ants 'R Awful" lotion for the ant bites? You and your Aunt Ethel have always seemed to attract those nasty fire ants.

   Now Tyler, I am very happy that you have met some new friends and that you are having fun together. However, you MUST stop trying to scare other campers. Remember, honey, some campers may frighten easily. I want you to apologize for any anxiety you may have caused them and start being the nice, polite boy that I know you are. Do you hear me, Tyler? Please be careful. I want you home safely.

                                                   Love,
                                                   Mom

Main idea _____

Dear Steven,   Saturday, June 7

    Camp is amazing this year! Our guides help us do the coolest stuff. Like yesterday, we hiked for six miles until we found this awesome spring. Then we used a rope hanging on a tree to jump in the water. I went so high that I made a huge splash! Thursday, our guides took us rowing. We rowed to this little island where we made a bonfire. We roasted the fish we had caught. My fish was the biggest, of course!

    Last night, we collected a big bunch of frogs in a bag. Then we put the bag under a bed in another cabin while they were all at the campfire. When they got back, the frogs were all over their cabin. We laughed so hard! I know they're going get us back. I've seen them planning. I can't wait to see what they try. Hey! How's the leg? Sure wish you were here!

Your friend,

Tyler

Main idea _____

Dear Tyler,   Tuesday, June 10

    That's great you're having so much fun! I wish I were there. All I do is sit around bumming out, thinking about all the fun you are having. I can't believe I broke my leg two days before camp started. My mom keeps renting me movies and video games, but I think I've seen everything and played everything. I just know I won't be happy again until this cast is off.

    Your new friends sound great! Sure wish I was there helping you guys play tricks on the other campers. Remember last year when we smeared honey all over another cabin and all those bees came? That was so funny—except the part where we had to scrub all the cabins clean wearing hot, protective gear. I'm still surprised they let you come back this summer!

    Hey! What's up with all the bugs? Your mom called my mom all worried about a bunch of bugs or something. Have fun and write soon!

Your friend,

Steven

Main idea _____

 Read a newspaper article about a foreign place. On another sheet of paper, write the main idea for each paragraph.

Super Duper Lance

The **main idea** tells what a story or paragraph is mostly about.
Details in a story provide the reader with information about
the main idea and help the reader better understand the story.

Lance Armstrong is an awesome athlete! This American bicyclist won the Tour de France bicycle race for seven consecutive years, from 1999 to 2005. What makes Armstrong's accomplishment even more amazing is that he was battling cancer before competing in the 1999 Tour de France race.

In 1996, Armstrong was diagnosed with cancer. This challenging disease was advancing rapidly. He was given only a 50% chance to live. Armstrong was faced with serious operations. In 1997, Armstrong received great news—he had won the race against cancer! This incredible athlete went on to win seven straight Tour de France races.

The Tour de France is the world's premier cycling event. It takes its competitors all over France, even through the Alps and the Pyrenees Mountains. The course changes each year but is always over 2,000 miles long and always ends in Paris.

Circle the main idea for each paragraph.

1. **Paragraph 1:**

   a. Armstrong was the first American bicyclist to win the Tour de France.

   b. Armstrong is an accomplished bicyclist.

   c. Armstrong rides all over France in the summer.

2. **Paragraph 2:**

   a. Armstrong was the first American bicyclist to win the Tour de France.

   b. Armstrong had cancer in 1996.

   c. Armstrong won an important "health" race.

3. **Paragraph 3:**

   a. Riders in the Tour de France get to see all of France.

   b. Tour de France competitors must be very strong to ride through two mountainous regions.

   c. The impressive Tour de France runs all over France and ends in Paris.

4. Use details from the story to write why you think Armstrong is an accomplished

   athlete. _____

   _____

   _____

   _____

   _____

   _____

5. Write a detail about the Tour de France bicycle race on each tire.

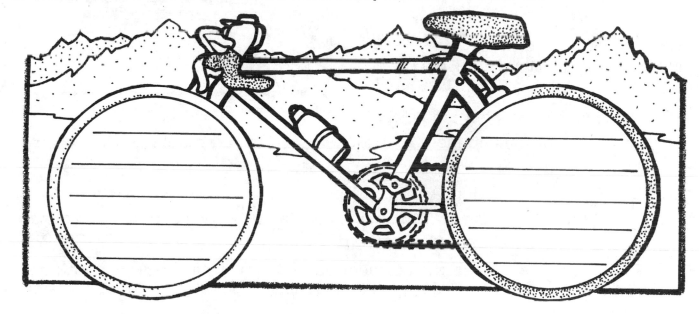

6. What are some of the challenges Armstrong has faced? Which one do you think

   was the most difficult? _____

   _____

   _____

   _____

 **Read a magazine article about another sports figure. On another sheet of paper, write
the main idea of the article.**

Honoring Heroes

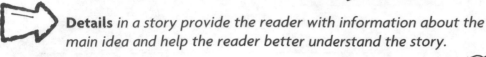

Details *in a story provide the reader with information about the main idea and help the reader better understand the story.*

Washington, D.C., is the capital of the United States. It is located between Virginia and Maryland on the Potomac River. Washington, D.C., is also the headquarters of the federal government. This incredible city is a symbol of our country's history and the home of many important historical landmarks.

Many of Washington, D.C.'s, famous landmarks are located in the National Mall. The Mall is a long, narrow, park-like area that provides large open spaces in the middle of the city's many huge buildings. In addition to being home to the U.S. Capitol, where Congress meets, and the White House, the Mall is also dedicated to honoring the history of our nation. Memorials for presidents George Washington, Abraham Lincoln, Thomas Jefferson, and Franklin D. Roosevelt can all be found in the Mall. There are also memorials honoring Americans who fought in the Korean and Vietnam Wars.

Near the Lincoln Memorial another memorial was built. It is the National World War II Memorial. This memorial honors Americans who fought and supported the United States during World War II. The U.S. fought in this war from 1941 to 1945.

The memorial features a Rainbow Pool, two giant arches, a ring of stone columns, and a wall covered with gold stars. Each star represents 100 Americans who died while fighting in World War II.

Bob Dole, a former senator and World War II veteran, worked tirelessly to get this memorial built. He believes that the memorial will remind Americans of the value of freedom. "Freedom is not free," says Dole. "It must be earned . . ."

More than $197 million was raised to build the memorial that means so much to Dole and to many other Americans. Many businesses, private groups, and schools donated money to this cause. The memorial was completed in 2004.

1. Where is Washington, D.C., located? _____

   _____

2. Write three facts about Washington, D.C. _____

   _____

   _____

3. Which four presidents are memorialized in the National Mall? _____

   _____

4. Besides the four presidents, who else is honored in the Mall? _____

   _____

5. What is the name of the memorial? _____

   _____

6. Why was it built? _____

   _____

7. How long did the United States fight in World War II? _____

8. What are some features of the memorial? _____

   _____

9. Write what the stars represent. _____

   _____

10. What World War II veteran has worked hard trying to get the memorial built? _____

    _____

11. What remembrance does Dole think the memorial will bring to the minds

    of people? _____

    _____

11. What are the sources of the money that was raised to build the memorial? _____

    _____

 Read about another memorial in Washington, D.C. On another sheet of paper, write five details about the memorial.

A Very Colorful House

 Context clues *are words or sentences that can help determine the meaning of a new word.*

Jackson was excited! He and his family were on their way to the White House. Jackson could not wait to see the President's official **residence**. He had been reading all about it so that he might recognize some things he saw. After standing in a long line, Jackson, his sister, and their parents were allowed to enter the 132-room, six-floor **mansion**. They entered through the East **Wing**. Jackson knew that he and his family were only four of the 6,000 people who would visit this **incredible** house that day.

The first room they were shown by the **guide** was the State Dining Room. Jackson learned that 140 dinner guests could eat there at one time. "What a great place for a huge birthday party!" Jackson thought.

The Red Room was shown next. Red satin **adorned** its walls. The third room the **visitors** entered was the Blue Room. This room serves as the main **reception** room for the President's guests. Jackson wondered when the President would be out to greet him. After all, he was a guest, too.

The Green Room was the fourth room on the **tour**. Jackson and his family were not surprised to find green silk covering the walls in this room.

The last room was the biggest room in the White House. It is called the East Room. Here, guests are **entertained** after **formal** dinners. Jackson wondered if they could **vary** the entertainment by rolling in **huge** movie screens so they could all watch the latest movies. He wondered if kids were invited sometimes; maybe they had huge, bouncy boxes you could jump in. Perhaps they even set up huge ramps so all the kids could practice skateboarding and roller blading. How fun!

Jackson loved his tour of the White House. He was just sorry that he did not get to see the living quarters of the President's family. He wondered if the President had to make *his* bed every day!

Write one of the bolded words from the story to match each definition below. Use context clues to help. Then write each numbered letter in the matching blank below to answer the question and learn an interesting fact.

1. following the usual rules or customs In an exact way __ __ __ __ __ __ __ __ __
   ₁

2. home __ __ __ __ __ __ __ __
   12   10

3. a gathering at which guests are received __ __ __ __ __ __ __ __ .
   9   17

4. kept interested with something enjoyable __ __ __ __ __ __ __ __ __ __ __
   15   16   8

5. decorated __ __ __ __ __ __ __
   13

6. a leader of a tour __ __ __ __ __
   4

7. a part that sticks out from a main part __ __ __ __
   2

8. a very large, stately house __ __ __ __ __
   7

9. a trip to inspect something __ __ __ __ __
   6

10. amazing __ __ __ __ __ __ __ __
    11

11. very large __ __ __ __
    5

12. guests __ __ __ __ __ __ __
    3

13. to change __ __ __ __ __
    14   18

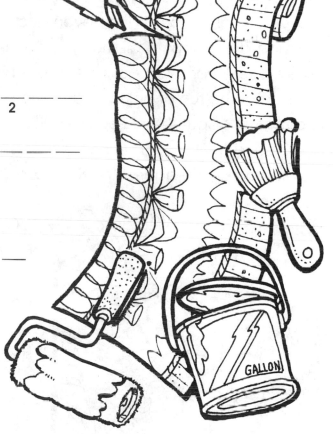

How many gallons of paint does it take to paint the outside of the White House?

__ __ __ __   __ __ __ __ __ __ __   __ __ __ __ __ __ __
1 2 3 4   5 6 7 8 9 10 11   12 13 14 15 16 17 18

Rattle! Rattle!

Many kids think Cassidy is crazy! That is okay with her. Cassidy loves rattlesnakes, and that is that. She has every book there is about these fascinating creatures. She loves seeing these animals in the zoo.

Rattlesnakes are extremely poisonous. They often use the rattle in their tails to give a warning sound before they strike. They are classed as pit vipers.

Cassidy has decided her favorite kind of rattlesnake is a diamondback rattlesnake. These snakes can grow to be over seven and one-half feet long! These large rattlesnakes are the most dangerous of all snakes, and they do not always rattle before striking. Like most rattlesnakes, diamondbacks like to eat birds and small mammals.

Part of the fun of being enamored with rattlesnakes is learning all kinds of interesting information about them. For example, Cassidy had always heard that you can tell the age of a rattler by the number of rattles in its tail. This, she learned, is not true. Two to four segments are added to the tail each year, one every time the rattler sheds its skin.

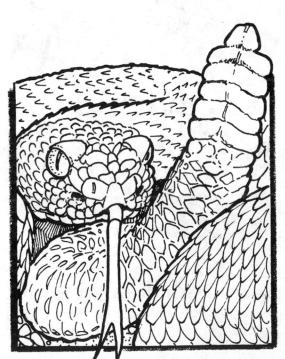

However, once ten have accumulated, they begin to fall off! So you can never be quite sure just how old a rattlesnake is!

Sometimes Cassidy's mom wishes her daughter could love kittens or puppies or ponies instead of poisonous snakes. But actually, Cassidy's love for snakes is definitely what makes her unique.

Name _____

Find a word in the snake to match each definition.

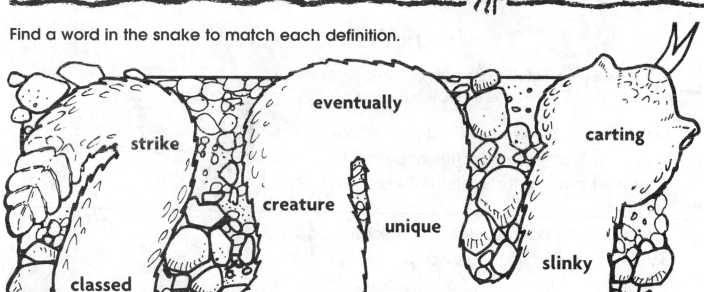

strike

eventually

carting

creature

unique

classed

slinky

fascinating

accumulated

enamored

1. classified _____
2. one of a kind _____
3. interesting _____
4. to attack _____
5. in love _____
6. sometime _____
7. collected _____
8. transporting _____
9. sleek _____
10. any person or animal _____

11. Check the main idea of the story.
    ☐ Cassidy wants a long snake.
    ☐ Cassidy loves large, dangerous rattlesnakes.
    ☐ Rattlesnakes do not always rattle before striking.

12. What kind of snake does Cassidy like best?

_____

Read an article about an animal that fascinates you. Choose five words from the article and write the definition of each on another sheet of paper.

America's First People

*To **compare** and **contrast** ideas in a passage, determine how the ideas are alike and how they are different.*

Native Americans were the first people to live in America. They lived in many different areas of the United States including the Eastern Woodlands and the Southwest.

The Eastern Woodlands Native Americans had a much different lifestyle than those who lived in the Southwest. The Eastern Woodlands encompassed all of the area from what is now the Canadian border down to the Gulf Coast. The area also extended from the East Coast to the Mississippi River. The northern parts of this area had cold winters, and the whole region had warm summers.

The Southwest Native Americans lived in a large, warm, dry area. Today, Arizona, New Mexico, southern Colorado, and northern Mexico make up this area. In the northern part of this region, wind and water created steep-walled canyons, sandy areas, mesas, buttes, and other interesting landforms. In the southern part, the desert land was flat and dry.

The Iroquois, Wampanoag, Cherokee, and Chickasaw are just a few of the major tribes that made their home in the Eastern Woodlands. The Southwest was home to tribes such as the Apache, Navajo, and Pueblo.

Housing was very different for the Native Americans who lived in these two different regions. The Eastern Woodlands natives built a variety of homes, depending on their location. Northern dwellers lived in dome-shaped wigwams covered with sheets of bark or in longhouses. A longhouse was a large, rectangular shelter that was home to a number of related families, each living in its own section. Those in the southeastern area often built villages around a central public square where community events took place.

Many of the Native Americans of the Southwest lived in cliff houses or large, many-storied homes built from rock and a mud-like substance called adobe. These adobe dwellings could house many families.

All of the Native Americans living in both regions ate a lot of corn, beans, and squash. Hunting was important in both regions, but fishing was more significant in the Eastern Woodlands.

The tribes living in both regions were excellent craftspeople. Those in the Eastern Woodlands made pottery, wicker baskets, and deerskin clothing. Many tribes in the Southwest also made pottery and were very skilled at spinning cotton and weaving it into cloth. This cloth was made into breechcloths and cotton kilts for the men and a kind of dress for the women.

Learning about these fascinating people is important as they have played, and continue to play, a valuable role in our country's history.

1. **Fill in the Venn diagram using the descriptions below.**

wigwams and longhouses	excellent craftspeople
made pottery	cold winters, warm summers
hunting	buttes
many-storied homes	Arizona, New Mexico, and southern Colorado
steep-walled canyons	corn, beans, and squash
fishing	Iroquois and Cherokee
Apache and Navajo	bordered what is now Canada

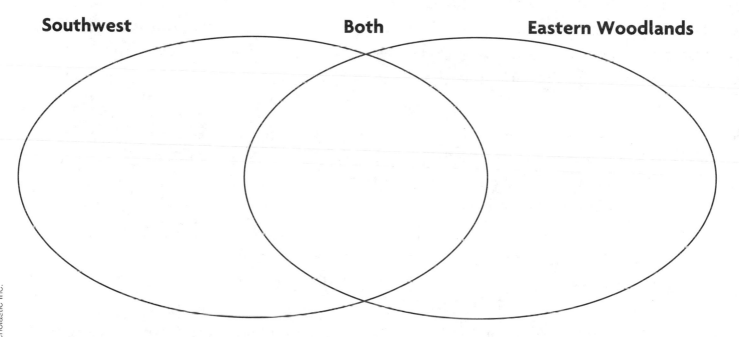

Southwest   **Both**   **Eastern Woodlands**

2. **Circle the ways longhouses and adobe houses were alike.**

    large   one-family dwellings   fairly small   multiple-family dwellings

3. **How was the climate in certain parts of the Eastern Woodlands different from other**

    parts in the same region? _____

    _____

A Difficult Choice

Emily and Zach are confused! Their parents told them they could choose between Massachusetts and Arizona for their vacation this summer, and they think both states seem pretty awesome. Emily has always wanted to visit Boston, the capital of Massachusetts. Zach and she both agree that strolling along the Freedom Trail would be pretty neat. Walking the trail would enable them to see Boston's most famous historic landmarks, like the site of the school Ben Franklin attended and the Old State House. It was built in 1713 and served as the seat of the colonial government.

Emily and Zach both love the beach. If they went to Massachusetts, they could spend a few days at the beaches on Cape Cod. Emily loves boogie boarding, and Zach is great at body surfing. They both enjoy building sandcastles with their mom and dad.

Zach finds learning about Native Americans fascinating and has always wanted to travel along the Apache Trail in Arizona. This mountain highway passes Native American ruins in Tonto National Forest. Emily is not as interested in traveling along this trail as Zach, but they both would like to visit Phoenix, the capital, and then travel to Grand Canyon National Park and Meteor Crater. Zach learned in science class that Meteor Crater is a hole over 4,000 feet wide and 520 feet deep that was created when a huge object from space fell to Earth. The object went so deep that it has never been found. Zach would really like to try to locate it. Emily thinks he is crazy! If experienced scientists and researchers cannot find it, Zach might as well not even bother to try.

If Arizona is the chosen state, Emily and Zach would also like to stop at a few other places. Arizona is home to fifteen national monuments. That is more than any other state.

The only drawback for Zach if they choose Arizona would be the heat. It is very hot and dry in this southwestern state. Arizona has a lot of what Massachusetts does not—desert land. Once in July in Arizona, it got up to 127°F !

Massachusetts, on the other hand, is located in the northeastern United States. Here, Zach and Emily and their parents could enjoy mild temperatures of about 75° F. Their parents love hot weather, but Zach and Emily do not really like to sweat. Therefore, both know that they would prefer the climate of Massachusetts.

How will they ever decide to which state they should travel? If only they could take two trips!

Name _____

1. "Pack" each suitcase to describe the two regions.

   Tonto National Forest

   Old State House

   Freedom Trail

   mild climate

   Phoenix

   Boston

   very hot

   Cape Cod

   Apache Trail

   Grand Canyon

2. Circle things both Emily and Zach like or would like to see.

building sandcastles	Apache Trail	hot weather	beach
Meteor Crater	surfboarding	Freedom Trail	sweating

3. Write one way Zach and Emily are different from their parents. _____

   _____

4. Write one way the Freedom Trail and the Apache Trail are different. _____

   _____

   _____

5. How do Zach and Emily spend their time differently at the beach? _____

   _____

6. How are Zach and Emily's feelings different when it comes to finding the missing

   object at Meteor Crater? _____

   _____

 Read about a state you would like to visit. On another sheet of paper, write five differences between the state you chose and the state in which you live.

A Real Cool Cowboy

 *The events in a story take place in a certain order. This is the **sequence** of events.*

Pecos Bill is a well-known character in American folklore. His legend developed from a magazine article written by Edward O'Reilly in 1923. This cowboy hero is often credited for being the creator of branding, roping, and other cowboy activities. It is also said that Pecos Bill taught broncos how to buck and cowboys how to ride.

Legend has it that Pecos Bill was born in the 1830s in Texas. He teethed on a bowie knife and had bears and other wild animals as friends. On a family trip to the West, little Bill fell out of the wagon near the Pecos River. He was found by coyotes that raised him.

Two famous natural landmarks are also amusingly traced back to Pecos Bill—the Grand Canyon and Death Valley. Supposedly, Pecos Bill once made a bet that he could ride an Oklahoma cyclone without a saddle. The cyclone was not able to throw him off, and it finally "rained out" under him in Arizona. This rain was so heavy that it created the Grand Canyon. When he reached California, Pecos Bill crashed. It was the force of his fall that is said to have created Death Valley. In actuality, some rocks in the deepest part of the Grand Canyon date back to about two billion years ago. The Colorado River began forming the Grand Canyon about six million years ago. Over centuries, the water eroded

the layers of rock, and the walls of the canyon were created. More erosion occurred later as a result of wind, rain, and melting snow. Death Valley is a desert in California and Nevada. It contains the lowest point in the Western Hemisphere at 282 feet below sea level.

No one is quite sure how Pecos Bill died. One version says he laughed himself to death after listening to silly questions a man from Boston asked him about the West.

1. Look at each picture. Number the events in the order in which they happened in the story. Write a sentence for each.

_____ _____ _____

_____ _____ _____

_____ _____ _____

_____ _____ _____

_____ _____ _____

_____ _____ _____

2. Four words from the story are hidden in the puzzle. The definition of each word is given below. Shade in the letters for each word, reading left to right and top to bottom. The remaining letters will spell the name of a real cool cowboy two times.

a piece of writing

laughingly

attributed with

a particular form of something

a	p	r	t	e	i	c
c	o	l	e	s	a	b
m	u	s	i	i	n	l
g	l	y	l	c	p	r
e	d	e	i	t	c	e
o	d	v	s	e	b	r
i	s	l	l	i	o	n

 Read a story about an imaginary character. On another sheet of paper, write five events from the character's life in the order in which they happened.

Fooled You!

Maria decided to have a Prank Party for her friends on April Fools' Day. She invited five of her best friends to come over for the afternoon. Maria and her mom made some delicious "pranks" for her party. They made treats that looked like one food but tasted like another. For example, Maria and her mom made fried-egg sundaes. These sweet treats looked like a fried egg in a bowl, but they were really made of vanilla ice cream topped with marshmallow fluff and a round blob of yellow pudding.

Another treat looked like a thin-crust pizza with vegetables. However, it was really a tortilla with strawberry and apricot jam, a black licorice stick, a green fruit roll, white chocolate chips, and cashew halves. It was so easy to make that Maria's little brother, Juan, even helped.

To make a "pizza," Juan and Maria first stirred the two jams together. Then Maria spread the jam on a tortilla, being careful not to go all the way to the edge. Maria's mom sliced the licorice stick to resemble black olives and the fruit roll to look like green pepper strips. The cashew halves looked like mushrooms.

Next, Maria melted the white chocolate chips at half power in the microwave for one-minute intervals. Juan stirred the chips after each minute to see if they were completely melted. (Maria's mom made sure he had a dry spoon when he stirred because she said that water makes the chocolate lose its creaminess.) Once it was melted, Maria quickly spread the melted chocolate on the pizza. Then she and Juan topped the "pizza" with the "olives," "peppers," and "mushrooms."

Maria's friends loved the delicious pranks she had made. No one dared to play an April Fool's trick on Maria since her pranks were so tasty and fun!

1. **Number the steps in the order Maria and Juan made a Prank Pizza.**

    ___ Juan and Maria topped the pizza.

    ___ Maria's mom created "olives" and "green peppers."

    ___ Maria melted the white chocolate chips.

    ___ Maria spread the jam on the tortillas.

    ___ Juan and Maria stirred the two jams together.

    ___ Juan stirred the chips with a dry spoon.

    ___ Maria spread the melted chocolate on the pizza.

2. On the pizzas below, write one way a real pizza is similar to Maria's Prank Pizza and one way it is different from it.

Similar 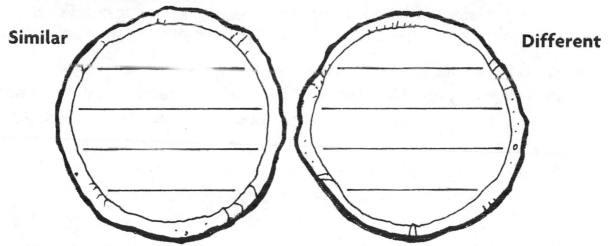 **Different**

3. Write a synonym from the story for each word below.
   trick _____
   celebration _____
   scrumptious _____

4. Why did Maria's mom make sure Juan used a dry spoon to stir the chocolate?

   _____

5. Check the ingredients used in making the Prank Pizza.
   ___ crust   ___ strawberries   ___ tortilla
   ___ apricot jam   ___ red licorice   ___ green fruit roll
   ___ walnuts   ___ cashews   chocolate chips

6. Circle the main idea of paragraph one.
   Maria is a big prankster.
   Maria "sweetly" tricked her friends on April Fools' Day.
   Maria's mom had great prank ideas for April Fools' Day.

7. What ingredients were in the fried-egg sundaes?

   _____

8. If the vegetables on Maria's pizza were real, what would they have been?

   _____

 Read the recipe of one of your favorite foods. Write each step on a strip of paper. Mix up the strips and then see if you can put them in the correct sequence.

A Happy Hero

 *To better understand a character, a reader needs to carefully study, or **analyze**, a character's traits, personality, motivations, relationships, and strengths and weaknesses.*

One day, Lindsay and Erica were sitting at Lindsay's house working very diligently. Fourth grade was tough, and they were working on a science project about weather. Lindsay was a hard worker like Erica, so the two girls were happy to have each other as partners. They were currently writing about rain and were amazed to learn that Hawaii is the world's wettest place. Lindsay found that Mount Waialeale, on the island of Kauai, gets about 460 inches of rain a year! In 1982, Mount Waialeale set an all-time world record when it received 666 inches of rain. The girls knew that their classmates would find all these facts interesting.

The girls were enjoying the fun facts they were finding when all of a sudden, Lindsay saw Erica choking. Erica had been chewing on a pen cap and had accidentally swallowed it! Erica started pointing to her neck. Lindsay asked her if she was choking. When Erica nodded to say yes, Lindsay quickly stood up and did the Heimlich maneuver to try to help Erica stop choking. (The Heimlich maneuver is a way to save someone from choking. This method is named after the doctor who invented it, Henry Heimlich.)

Lindsay was afraid of hurting her friend, so the first time she tried the Heimlich maneuver, she did not do it very hard. She tried a second time, and nothing happened. After trying it a third time, the pen cap flew out of Erica's mouth!

Erica was very grateful to Lindsay. She had been terrified when she realized she had swallowed the pen cap and could not breathe. Lindsay was very brave to try to save her friend. This was one science project that both girls would never forget!

Name _____

1. Circle each word that describes Lindsay.

   hard worker   boring   brave   fast-thinking

   quick-acting   selfish   timid   lazy

2. Circle each word that tells how Erica might have been feeling when she realized
   she was choking.

   scared   thankful   enthusiastic   helpless

   courageous   sick   alarmed   friendly

3. What do you think Lindsay might be when she grows up? _____

   _____

4. Write *L* for Lindsay, *E* for Erica, or *B* for both.

   ____ good students   ____ frightened   ____ persistent

   ____ courageous   ____ grateful   ____ appreciative

5. What is the name of the doctor who invented the lifesaving maneuver?

   _____

6. What is the name of the wettest place in the world? _____

7. Circle the average amount of rain Mount Waialeale received each day in 1982.

   almost 3"   just under 2"   just over 4"   about 1"

8. Why do you think this project will be one neither girl will ever forget? _____

   _____

   _____

 **Choose a character from a book. On another sheet of paper, make a list of ten words
that describe this character.**

A New Team for Juan

Juan was angry! His mom had signed him up late for baseball, and now he was not on his old team. He would not get to play with Tyler, Joe, and Brad. They had played together for four years! And they all loved Coach Dave—he was one of the best coaches in the league. Juan was not even sure if he wanted to play at all. He just knew it would not be any fun.

At the first practice, Juan walked slowly to the field. He saw one guy pitching and one hitting. The guy hitting struck out. "Great!" thought Juan. "I will be on a team with no hitters!" Juan continued on to the field. He saw some guys playing catch. One guy missed an easy ball. "Perfect!" thought Juan. "I will also have to teach them how to catch!"

Juan thought about calling it quits when he suddenly realized that Eric, a friend from school, was on the team. Eric was a great pitcher! "Well, maybe I will stay for a bit," Juan said to himself.

Juan started looking around some more. He recognized two other kids he had watched when he had been on the other team. One was a fast runner, and one never missed a pop fly. "Hey! This team might be okay after all!" thought Juan.

Eric was excited to see Juan. "Hey, Juan! I'm glad you are on our team. We are going to have a great team. Do you know who our coach is?"

Juan was sure the coach would not be as good as Coach Dave, but Eric was excited. "So, who is the coach, Eric?" Juan asked, somewhat indifferently.

"It's Home Run Harvey!" Eric replied excitedly.

"Home Run Harvey!" exclaimed Juan. "The one and only Home Run Harvey from the university team?"

"That is right," said Eric. "His little brother is on our team, and he wants to coach." Juan could not believe how lucky he was to get on Home Run Harvey's team!

"So who is his brother?" Juan asked.

"Tim is over there," said Eric, pointing to the guy who had not caught what Juan had called an "easy ball."

Juan felt badly for thinking negatively about Tim's missed catch. Everyone misses a ball now and then. Juan could not wait to tell his friends about his new team and coach!

1. Check how Juan felt in each situation.

He could not play baseball with his friends.

He sees a player on his new team strike out.

He sees his friend, Eric.

He learns Home Run Harvey is the coach.

	positive	negative

2. Why was Juan angry that he could not play on his old team? _____

_____

3. Underline when Juan first started feeling more positive about the new team.

when he saw a player who was a fast runner

when he saw a player who never missed a pop fly

when he saw Eric

4. Why do you think Juan felt badly about what he thought when he saw Tim miss

a catch? _____

5. Circle the words that describe Juan at the end of the story.

angry   scared   excited   pessimistic   remorseful   timid

6. Circle the main idea of the story.

Juan's mom made a terrible mistake, and now Juan had to suffer.

What Juan thought was going to be a negative experience soon looked
like it could be a positive one.

Juan is going to get awesome coaching from a very talented ball player.

7. What kind of season do you think Juan's team will have? _____

_____

_____

Choose three characters from a book. On another sheet of paper, write two different
words to describe each character.

Such Choices

 Making predictions *is using information from a story to determine what will happen next.*

Hurray! Spring break is here! Tommy's mom and dad are also on vacation from work all week. They want to plan all kinds of fun things to do, like biking, hiking, fishing, swimming, and tennis. They are hoping for some warm, enjoyable weather. However, they just cannot decide which day to do each activity. So, they decided to check the weather forecast in the newspaper before making some final plans.

THE FIVE-DAY FORECAST

Monday	Tuesday	Wednesday	Thursday	Friday
a beauty with no clouds; high of 82	partly cloudy with a 40% chance of afternoon thunderstorms; high of 80	lingering showers until noon; then clearing and cooler with a high of 70	partly sunny with a high of 60	partly cloudy with a high of 65

1. Tommy and his dad want to spend one whole day fishing. On which day(s) might they not want to go fishing? _____

2. What day would be the best day for swimming? _____

3. What other activities could Tommy and his family do on Tuesday and Wednesday?

_____

_____

4. On what days do you think the family might wear jeans and jackets? _____

_____

5. Do you think Tommy and his family are pleased with the forecast? Why or why not?

_____

_____

6. To do the kinds of activities Tommy and his family want to do, which forecast do you think they would like to see every day of spring break? Why?

_____

_____

7. Write the word from the forecast that means "staying." _____

8. Circle the words that describe Tommy's family.

    incompetent   athletic   energetic   listless

9. Circle the things Tommy and his family might want to take with them if they go swimming on Monday.

    jacket   goggles   sunglasses

    cooler with drinks   rain umbrella   sunscreen

10. Write a paragraph about what Tuesday might be like for Tommy.

_____

_____

_____

_____

 Read the weather forecast in the newspaper. Choose four different cities in the country. On another sheet of paper, make a list of the activities you could do in each city, based on the forecast. What other information did you use to make your list?

A New Start

 *Every story has certain **story elements**. These elements include the characters, the setting, the problem, and the solution.*

In the late 1500s, brave men and women and their children sailed from Europe across the Atlantic Ocean to America, looking for a better way of life. These people wanted better jobs than they had in their homelands, and many wanted the freedom to choose their own religion. Still others wanted the opportunity to be able to buy land.

This period of time in America is known as the colonial period. It lasted about 170 years. During this time, many colonists worked very hard creating a new nation. The first colony, Jamestown, was established in 1607. Between 1607 and 1733, 13 permanent colonies were established on the east coast of America. These colonies started to grow and prosper as more and more people from other countries began to immigrate. As the population of the colonies grew, trade and manufacturing developed quickly, especially in towns that had good harbors.

Despite the growth and the many successes of the colonies, the colonists also faced their fair share of problems. One very big problem was the friction between the colonies and Britain. The colonists wanted very much to control themselves and have more say in making decisions that affected them. However, the British Parliament would not allow it. This angered the colonists, so they often ignored British laws.

As Britain imposed more and more taxes on the colonists, the colonists grew angrier and angrier. Acts passed by Parliament, such as the Sugar Act and the Stamp Act, forced the colonists to take action against Britain.

In 1774, delegates from all the colonies except Georgia met to decide how to gain some independence from Britain. Their attempts failed. They met again in 1775. The delegates helped organize an army and a navy to fight the British soldiers. The colonists wanted freedom from Britain. They outlined this freedom on July 4, 1776, in the Declaration of Independence.

Name _____

List each story element.

main characters: _____

setting: _____

problem: _____

solution: _____

Use words from the story to complete the puzzle.

Across

1. Britain _____ many taxes on the colonists, which greatly angered them.

7. People from other countries, looking for better jobs or religious freedom, would _____ to America.

8. The colonies decided they wanted to gain _____ from Britain.

Down

2. Thirteen _____ colonies were established in America between 1607 and 1733.

3. _____ from almost all of the colonies met to discuss how to gain independence from Britain.

4. The colonists tried to organize an army and a navy to fight the British _____ .

5. The men, women, and children who left their countries to come to America were very _____ .

6. There was _____ between the American colonies and Britain.

9. As people from other countries moved to America, the colonies started to grow and _____ .

On another sheet of paper, list the story elements from your favorite movie.

A "Peachy" Beach Day

 *The **cause** is what makes something happen.*
*The **effect** is what happens as a result of the cause.*

The day was beautiful! Janie and Jake's mom decided to take them to the beach. She even told them that since they had finished their chores without complaining, they could each bring a friend. Janie and Jake were excited! They loved the beach.

Janie decided to ask Hayley to go since Hayley had just had her over to play last week. Jake asked his friend Charlie— they went everywhere together. Once both friends had arrived, it was time to load up the van. The kids packed some beach toys they might want—shovels, buckets, beach balls, and flippers. Mom packed a cooler with sandwiches and drinks, towels, sunscreen, and a chair for herself.

On the way to the beach, Jake and Charlie groaned. They had forgotten their boogie boards. Oh well! At least they had buckets and shovels they could use to build a huge sandcastle. Jake and Charlie loved to see how big they could make a sandcastle. They even liked to add roads and moats and lots of other details.

Once they reached the beach, everyone helped unload and set up. Then Mom put sunscreen on everyone. It was going to be a hot one—91° with no clouds! Everyone even put on hats.

Right away, the kids started playing. Jake and Charlie started working on their sandcastle, and Janie and Hayley went looking for shells. What a great day!

1. **By each cause, write the letter of the effect.**

   Cause:

   ____ It was a beautiful, hot day.

   ____ They forgot their boogie boards.

   ____ Jake and Charlie go everywhere together.

   Effect:

   A. Jake asked Charlie to go to the beach.

   B. Mom put sunscreen on all the kids.

   C. Jake and Charlie were disappointed.

2. Write *C* for cause or *E* for effect for each pair of sentences.

   a. ____ Mom decided to take the kids to the beach.

      ____ The day was beautiful.

   b. ____ They forgot their boogie boards.

      ____ Jake and Charlie would be building sandcastles instead of
         boogie boarding.

   c. ____ Janie and Jake each got to take a friend to the beach.

      ____ The children finished their chores without complaining.

   d. ____ Janie asked Hayley to go with her to the beach.

      ____ Hayley had just had Janie over to play.

3. Circle the main idea of the first paragraph.

   Janie and Jake loved to go to the beach.

   Janie and Jake finished their chores without complaining.

   Since it was a beautiful day, Janie and Jake's mom was taking them to
   the beach.

4. Janie and Jake each asked a friend to go to the beach for a different reason.
   Write each child's reason on the correct sandcastle.

Janie   Jake

5. What might Hayley or Charlie have thought on the way home from the beach?

   _____

   _____

 **Simon had to miss baseball practice last night. On another sheet of paper, write three
possible causes for this effect.**

Planet Particulars

 *To make an **inference** is to figure out what is happening in a story from clues the author provides.*

There are nine planets that travel around the sun. They are much smaller than the sun and stars which are shining balls of hot gases. The sun and stars produce their own heat and light. The planets do not produce heat or light. They get almost all of their heat and light from the sun. Each planet has features which make it unique.

Sun Mercury Venus Earth Mars Jupiter Saturn Uranus Neptune Pluto

1. It takes _____ about 248 years to orbit the sun. It is a dwarf planet and is located next to Neptune.

2. The largest planet, _____, is the fifth planet from the sun. It is about 1,000 times bigger than Earth. Saturn is next to this planet.

3. _____ rotates while lying on its side. It takes about 84 years to orbit the sun. It is the seventh planet from the sun.

4. _____'s surface temperature is about 370° F below zero! Brrrrr! It is the eighth planet from the sun. It is located between Pluto and Uranus.

5. We live on _____, the third planet from the sun. It takes this planet 365 days to orbit the sun. It is often called the "living planet."

6. Many rings surround _____. It takes 10,759 days to orbit the sun. It is located between Uranus and Jupiter.

7. _____ is the closest planet to the sun. It is next to Venus, the second planet from the sun. This planet only takes 88 days to orbit the sun.

8. _____ is often called the "red planet." It lies between Earth and Jupiter, the largest planet. This planet has the largest volcano in the solar system— much higher than Mount Everest!

9. _____ was called the "mystery planet" for a long time because it is covered by thick clouds. It is the second planet from the sun.

Guess the State

Spencer, Jack, Grant, and Kara are new in Mrs. Sleen's fourth-grade class. Each of these students came from one of the following states: Pennsylvania, Arizona, Washington, and Massachusetts. They are taking turns giving the class clues about the state from which they moved. The other children are trying to guess the state from the clues.

Use the following clues to help you determine which state was the home of each new student. Write each new student's name on the correct state outline below. Label the state in which all the students now live.

1. Spencer is not from the Keystone State.

2. Grant is not from the south or the east.

3. Kara is not from the south or the west.

4. Jack is not from the south or the west.

5. Grant and Spencer are both from states that border another country.

6. Jack and Kara lived the closest to each other before they moved.

7. Grant used to be able to visit the Space Needle.

8. Many of Spencer's old friends speak Spanish very well.

9. Kara used to live in "the birthplace of the United States."

10. Jack used to vacation on Cape Cod. He also loved strolling along the Freedom Trail.

11. All four children love their new state. It is located in the northeastern corner of the United States. It is the largest New England state. Its nickname is the Pine Tree State. Canada forms its northern boundary.

Off to the City

Maura and her grandmother are going into the city today to run some errands and do some shopping. Maura loves spending time with her grandmother. The two of them always have so much to talk about. Maura loves to hear about all the funny things her grandmother did when she was Maura's age. They did some really interesting things way back then when there were no TV's. For example, Maura's grandmother used to play jacks. She and her best friend, Sue, were the best jacks players in their school.

At 10:00 A.M. sharp, Grandma pulled in the driveway to pick up Maura. She honked the horn as she always did on their big shopping days. This was the signal that they had a busy day ahead and could not waste any time.

Maura ran out to the car, dressed in the new jeans and top Grandma bought her on their last trip. Maura knew that Grandma loved to see Maura wearing the clothes she had bought her.

As expected, Grandma told Maura some more funny things she did when she was Maura's age. Today, she told Maura how she and Sue were so hungry for candy one day in July that they decided to put on a performance and charge admission. The two girls dressed up like clowns. Grandma said people laughed so hard that the two girls were able to buy all kinds of fun treats that day. Maura made a note to herself to definitely try that some day.

Before they knew it, Maura and Grandma were in the city. Grandma found a parking spot, and away they went to begin their big day!

1. **Why are Maura and Grandma going to the city?** _____

   _____

2. **List something Grandma did for fun when she was a girl. Compare it with something Maura might spend her time doing for fun.**

   _____

   _____

Help Maura and Grandma find their way around the city. Follow the directions to complete the map.

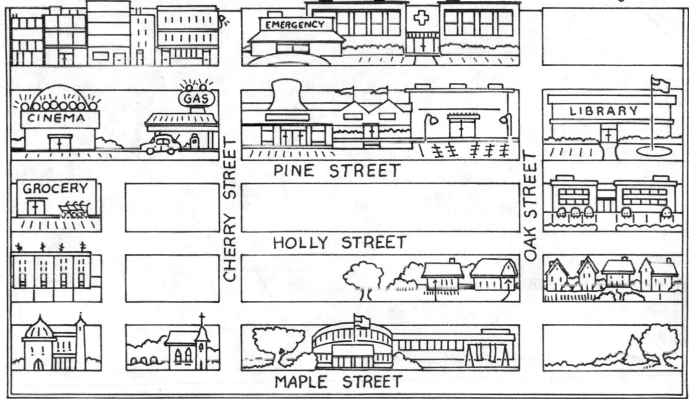

1. Maura wants to go to the mall first. It is just south of the hospital. Cherry Street runs along the western side of the mall. Label the mall.

2. On the southern side of Pine Street and the western side of Oak Street is Grandma's eye doctor. Draw a pair of eye glasses here.

3. There are five houses on Elm Street east of the hospital. Elm Street is south of the hospital. Label Elm Street and draw five houses across from the library.

4. The supermarket is located on the corner of Holly Street and Evergreen Street. Grandma needs some groceries. Label Evergreen Street.

5. There is a great park where Maura wants to play that is located between Maple and Pear streets. Oak Street runs north/south along the western side of the park. Label Pear Street, and draw three trees in the park.

6. The fire station is located on the western side of Cherry Street, north of Holly Street. Draw and label it.

7. The police station is located to the south of the fire department. Draw and label it.

 Draw a map that shows how to get from your house to your favorite fast-food restaurant.

Food for Fitness

 Classifying *means putting things into categories with other similar things.*

Katie knows that it is very important to eat right and to exercise in order to stay healthy. That is why she gets up every morning and has **oatmeal**, a **banana**, and a glass of **milk** for breakfast. Then Katie goes to play kickball.

Katie, Jimmy, Toni, and Anna always organize a two-on-two game of kickball. After playing all morning, the foursome usually sits down for lunch. Katie knows Toni's lunch by heart— **chicken nuggets**, **carrots** and dip, an **apple**, and two **chocolate chip cookies**. Jimmy's lunch varies a little. Some days it is **ham** on **wheat bread**, **grapes**, **yogurt**, and a **candy bar**. Other days his mom will make him come home to eat a good, hot meal of **peas** and **corn**, **rice**, a **hamburger**, **strawberries**, and homemade **ice cream**. Usually on those days, Jimmy has eaten **doughnuts** for breakfast.

The only meat Anna eats is fish, so she often has **fish sticks**, crunchy **broccoli**, a

pear, **cheese** and **crackers** and occasionally a piece of her mom's delicious **chocolate cake**. Katie always wants a bite of the cake. Sometimes Anna shares, and sometimes she does not.

To finish off her day of trying to eat healthy, Katie usually goes home to one of her dad's magnificent meals. Tonight they are having **pork chops**, **pasta**, **cauliflower** with cheese sauce, and her choice of turtle **cheesecake** or a **vanilla milk shake**. Although Katie and her friends eat some sweets, they try not to eat a lot of them, and they exercise each day.

Copyright © Scholastic Inc.

Name _____

Write each bolded word from the story in the chart under the correct category.

Dairy	Vegetables	Grains	Fruits	Meat & Fish	Fats/Sweets

1. What does Katie do to stay healthy? _____

2. Circle the foods Anna would NOT eat.

    hamburger   broccoli   apple   chicken   cheese   ribs   salmon

3. List four foods Katie might have had for a healthy lunch. _____

_____

4. Write C for Cause and E for Effect

    ___ Jimmy goes home to eat a good, hot meal.

    ___ Jimmy has probably eaten doughnuts for breakfast.

5. Write K for Katie, J for Jimmy, T for Toni, or A for Anna.

    ____ chocolate chip cookies   ____ fish sticks

    ____ candy bar   ____ chicken nuggets

    ____ banana   ____ ham

    ____ pear   ____ corn

    ____ carrots   ____ oatmeal

On another sheet of paper, list all the foods you eat in one day. Classify the foods.

Flower Fun

 To draw conclusions is to use the information in a story to make a logical assumption.

Aaaaaahhhhh! It was that time of year again— time to plant flowers. Christina and her dad were trying to decide what kind of flowers to plant this year. Her dad showed her an ad in the morning paper. He wanted Christina to check it out so she could help him determine what they should buy. The two always like to surprise Christina's mom with beautiful flowers before her "big day" in May. Christina was surprised to see Flower Power was having a sale. She knew they had better hurry to the store.

> FLOWER POWER SALE
> Beautiful flowers of all kinds — annuals and perennials— are all on sale — 25% OFF!
> All pots and hanging baskets are on sale, too Buy one, get one FREE!
> Reg. $3.99 to $49.99
> Hurry! Sale ends Tuesday!
> Flower Power
> 2418 Harbor Ave.

1. What time of year is it? _____

2. Circle the day in May on which Christina and her dad want her mother to enjoy beautiful flowers.

   Father's Day   Earth Day   Mother's Day   Easter

3. Circle why Christina and her dad will probably go to Flower Power today.

   because they are having a sale

   because they want to plant today

   because the two always plant flowers together

4. Why was Christina surprised that Flower Power was having a sale?

   _____

5. Why might Christina and her dad want to buy new pots or hanging baskets?

   _____

6. Why does the ad say to hurry? _____

   _____

   _____

On the Move

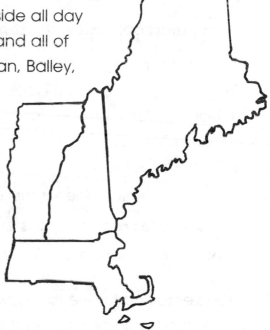

Sam and Danny cannot believe that they have to move away from Florida. Florida is so awesome! They can play outside all day long—every day. It is almost always warm and sunny, and all of their friends live there. What will they do without Brendan, Bailey, John, Alexis, and Brian? They will never have such great friends again. Never!

However, Sam and Danny are very excited for their dad. He has a great new job. The only problem is that the job is in New Hampshire. Danny was not even sure where this state was located. After learning that it is way up north near Canada, both boys did get a little excited about playing in the snow. Danny has always wanted to learn to ski, and Sam thinks playing ice hockey sounds like fun.

Sam and Danny also like the location of New Hampshire. It is between Maine and Vermont and not far from Boston, Massachusetts. Quebec, Canada, borders this state on the north. Neither of the boys has ever visited this part of the country, so they are now looking forward to exploring a new area. If only their friends could come with them! Their parents have promised that they can visit their old friends over spring break and even go to Disney World. The boys think that moving to New Hampshire will not be so bad after all.

1. **How do Sam and Danny feel about Florida?** _____

_____

2. **Circle how Sam and Danny feel about leaving their friends.**

   They are sad.

   They do not know what they will do without their good friends.

   They know they will make a lot of new friends.

3. **Circle how the boys feel about moving to New Hampshire.**

   They think it sounds like a fun, interesting part of the country.

   They are excited about visiting their old friends on spring break.

   They are disappointed that it is next to Vermont.

4. **On the map above, label New Hampshire and the country and states that border it.**

The Wonderful Whale

 *A **summary** tells the most important parts of a story.*

For each paragraph, circle the sentence that tells the most important part.

1. The largest animal that has ever lived is the blue whale. It can grow up to 300 feet long and weigh more than 100 tons. Whales, for the most part, are enormous creatures. However, some kinds only grow to be 10 to 15 feet long.

The blue whale is the largest animal.

Most whales are enormous creatures.

Some whales are only 10 to 15 feet long.

2. Whales look a lot like fish. However, whales differ from fish in many ways. For example, the tail fin of a fish is up and down; the tail fin of a whale is sideways. Fish breathe through gills. Whales have lungs and must come to the surface from time to time to breathe. Whales can hold their breath for a very long time. The sperm whale can hold its breath for about an hour.

Whales and fish do not share similar breathing patterns.

Whales can hold their breath for about an hour.

Whales might look a lot like fish, but the two are very different.

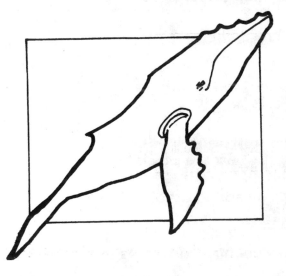

3. Baleen whales have no teeth. Toothed whales have teeth. Baleen whales have hundreds of thin plates in their mouth. They use these plates to strain out food from the water. Their diet consists of tiny plants and animals. Toothed whales eat such foods as other fish, cuttlefish, and squid.

Whales can be divided into two groups— baleen and toothed.

Baleen whales have plates in their mouths; toothed whales do not.

Toothed whales use their teeth to chew their food.

4.   Whales have a layer of fat called blubber. Blubber keeps them warm. Whales can live off their blubber for a long time if food is scarce. Blubber also helps whales float, as it is lighter than water.

   Layers of fat are called blubber.

   Blubber is very important to whales and has many purposes.

   Blubber is what makes whales float.

5. Write the main idea of each paragraph to complete a summary about whales.

   _____

   _____

   _____

   _____

   _____

6. Fill in the whale and the fish with the following descriptions. Write what the two have in common in the shared space. Write the descriptions that are specific to each on the spaces that don't overlap.

   can hold breath for long time   people love to watch

   gills   tail fin sideways

   live in ponds   tail fin up and down

   live in oceans   lungs

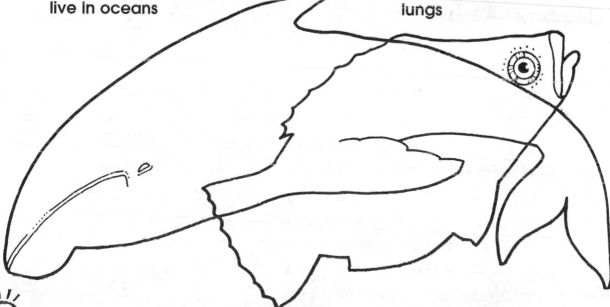

💡   **Read information about another animal. On another sheet of paper, write a summary of the information.**

Climbing Blindly

 A **fact** *is information that can be proven.*
(Example: Asia is a continent.)

*An **opinion** is information that tells what someone thinks.*
(Example: Asia is the most interesting continent in the world.)

Mount Everest is the highest mountain in the world. This mountain is located in Asia. Asia is home to all five of the world's highest mountains. Mount Everest's peak is five and one-half miles above sea level. That is very high!

Many climbers have tried to climb to the top of Mount Everest's approximately 29,141-foot peak. The first people to reach the peak were Sir Edmund Hillary and Tenzing Norgay. Since then, about 900 people have survived the climb to Mount Everest's top.

One of the successful climbers is Erik Weihenmayer. Like all who try to climb this huge mountain, Erik faced strong winds, snow, and avalanches. However, what really made Erik's

climb unbelievable is the fact that he is blind. After losing his vision at age 13, Erik began climbing at age 16. He has climbed the tallest mountains on five continents. Erik became the first blind person to reach the peak of Mount Everest.

At the age of 32, Erik began his climb as part of a 19-member team. His team wore bells that he could follow during his climb, and fellow climbers were quick to warn him of such things as a big drop on the right or a boulder to the left. Erik also used long climbing poles and an ice ax to feel his way across the ice, rock, and snow on the mountain.

During his climb, Erik encountered many dangers. He struggled through 100 m.p.h. winds and sliding masses of snow, ice, and rock. Because the air became thinner the higher Erik climbed, he wore an oxygen mask, as do many who climb high mountains. This helped him breathe as he climbed higher and higher. It took Erik about two-and-a half months to reach the top of this incredible mountain.

1. Write *F* for fact or *O* for opinion.

   ___ Erik is very courageous.

   ___ The bells made Erik's climb a lot easier.

   ___ Erik is blind.

   ___ All climbers should use climbing poles and ice axes.

   ___ Mount Everest is the world's tallest mountain.

   ___ Erik's oxygen mask helped him breathe.

   ___ Erik used tools to help him climb.

   ___ Erik is proud of his achievement.

2. List three interesting facts from the story. _____

   _____

   _____

3. Write your opinion of Erik's accomplishment. _____

   _____

   _____

4. Circle words that describe Erik.

   brave   foolish   cautious   strong   daring   athletic

5. What are some climbing tools many climbers use? _____

   _____

6. Do you think bells are a good idea for all teams of climbers to use? Why or

   why not? _____

   _____

   _____

7. Why do you think Erik attempted this dangerous climb? _____

   _____

   _____

**Read about another adventurous person. On another sheet of paper, write three facts
and three opinions about this person.**

Don't Worry, Be Happy

*Understanding an author's purpose when writing will make appreciating literature easier for the reader. Authors have a purpose when writing such as to **inform** (give readers facts), to **persuade** (convince readers to do or believe something), or to **entertain** (tell an interesting story).*

If I were a bird, I'd fly up high,
Above the clouds, up in the sky.
I'd float and sing and soar and play,
Without any worries to ruin my day.

If I were a dolphin, I'd splash in the sea,
And dive and flip—what fun for me!
I'd play with friends under the sea so blue.
There'd be no chores or homework to do.

If I were a bear, I'd sleep all day,
And then wake up at night to play.
I'd fish and run and jump and climb,
With no one around to ruin my good time.

If I were a dog, during the day I'd rest,
So when my master came home, I'd be at my best—
Ready to run or play ball or catch,
Ready to jump, roll over, or fetch.

But I'm not a dog or a bird or a bear.
I'm not a dolphin who can swim everywhere.
I'm just a kid who wants to have fun,
But I know I can't till my work's all done!

1. Circle why you think the author wrote this poem.

   to persuade   to inform   to entertain

2. Circle what you think the author is trying to tell you.

   The author wants to fly or swim or play all day.

   Working is not what the author would choose to do.

   The author wants to be an animal.

3. Circle why you think the author thinks about being something else.

   The author wants to escape from worries and work and be free like animals.

   The author wants a pet.

   The author would love to be an animal.

4. List three things the author wants to leave behind. _____

   _____   _____

5. Write the following words on the matching animal. Some words will be used more than once.

fly	play ball	splash	jump	climb	float	sing
sleep	run	play	flip	roll over	dive	fetch
soar	rest	fish	catch			

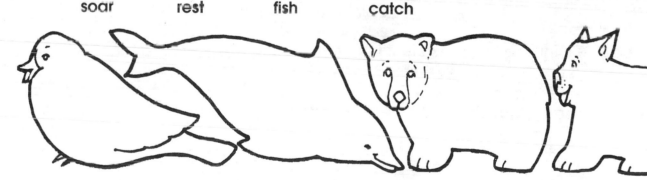

6. Write *F* for Fact or ○ for Opinion.

   ____ The author would like to escape worries and work like a bird or a dolphin.

   ____ The author is unhappy as a human and wants to be an animal.

   ____ The author knows work needs to be finished before playing.

   ____ The author just wants to have fun.

   ____ The author feels sorry for all kids who have to do work.

 Find three articles in a newspaper or magazine that are written for different purposes. Share the articles with a friend.

Improve Learning by Skating

I believe that all students should be able to roller blade during school. Roller blading would allow students to get around the school more quickly. This would leave more class time, and thus, students would learn more. It would also get the students outside quicker, so they could enjoy a longer recess. Because everyone would be moving quickly in the hallways, there would be no time for talking or messing around. The teachers would really like that!

Roller blading is a very good form of exercise. Just think of how physically fit every student would be! Being physically fit often leads to better health. Consequently, students would be absent less and would be learning more.

Finally, roller blading is fun. More learning, better physical fitness, and fun, I believe, are the keys to a successful school.

1. **Circle the author's purpose for writing this passage.**

   to persuade   to inform   to entertain

2. **Why do you think the author wrote this article?** _____

   _____

3. **List three reasons students should be allowed to roller blade during school.**

   _____

   _____

   _____

4. **List three reasons students should not be allowed to roller blade during school.**

   _____

   _____

   _____

 On another sheet of paper, write an article about a change you would like to see take place. Read the article to a friend.

Pages 4–5

Answers will vary. Sample main ideas: Letter one—Except for the bugs, Tyler and his new friends are having fun at camp.; Letter two—Tyler's mom is worried about his bug bites, and she wants him to start being nice to the other campers.; Letter Three—Tyler is having a great time at camp, has some new friends, and is having fun playing tricks on other campers.; Letter four—Steven is sad he could not go to camp and remembers the fun he had at camp last year.

Pages 6–7

1. b; 2. c; 3. c; 4. Answers will vary. 5. Answers will vary. Sample answers: The course for the Tour de France changes each year. The course is always over 2,000 miles long. 6. Armstrong faced the challenges of battling cancer and competing in the Tour de France. Opinions will vary.

Pages 8–9

1. between Virginia and Maryland on the Potomac River; 2. Answers will vary. Possible answers: capital of the United States, symbol of our country's history, home of many important historic landmarks; 3. George Washington, Abraham Lincoln, Thomas Jefferson, and Franklin D. Roosevelt; 4. Americans who fought in the Korean War and Vietnam War; 5. The National World War II Memorial; 6. to honor Americans who fought in World War II; 7. about four years—1941–1945; 8. Rainbow Pool, two giant arches, ring of stone columns, wall covered with stars; 9. Americans who died fighting in World War II; 10. Bob Dole; 11. the value of freedom; 12. many business, private groups, and schools

Pages 10–11

1. formal; 2. residence; 3. reception; 4. entertained; 5. adorned; 6. guide; 7. wing; 8. mansion; 9. tour; 10. incredible; 11. huge; 12. visitors; 13. vary; five hundred seventy

Pages 12–13

1. classed; 2. unique; 3. fascinating; 4. strike; 5. enamored; 6. eventually; 7. accumulated; 8. carting, 9. slinky, 10. creature, 11. Cassidy loves large, dangerous snakes. 12. a diamondback rattlesnake

Pages 14–15

1. Southwest: many-storied homes; steep-walled canyons; buttes; Arizona, New Mexico, and southern Colorado; Apache and Navajo; Both: made pottery; hunting; excellent craftspeople; corn, beans, and squash; Eastern Woodlands: wigwams and longhouses; fishing; cold winters, warm summers; Iroquois and Cherokee; bordered what is now Canada; 2. large, multiply-family dwellings; 3. The northern parts had cold winters.

Pages 16–17

1. Arizona. Tonto National Forest, Phoenix, very hot, Apache Trail, Grand Canyon; Massachusetts: Old State House, Freedom Trail, mild climate, Boston, Cape Cod; 2. building sandcastles, beach, Meteor Crater, Freedom Trail; 3. Their parents love hot weather. Zach and Emily do not. 4. You can walk on the Freedom Trail; you must drive along the Apache Trail. 5. Emily likes to boogie board, and Zach likes to body surf. 6. Zach thinks he might be able to find the missing object. Emily thinks he is crazy to think he might find it.

Pages 18–19

1. Picture order: 5, 1, 6, 3, 4, 2, Sentences will vary.
2.

a	p	r	t	e	i	c
c	o	l	e	s	a	b
m	u	s	i	i	n	l
g	l	y	l	c	p	r
e	d	e	i	t	c	e
o	d	v	s	e	b	r
i	s	l	l	i	o	n

Pages 20–21

1. 7, 3, 4, 2, 1, 5, 6; 2. Answers will vary. 3. prank, party, delicious; 4. because water makes the chocolate lose its creaminess; 5. tortilla, apricot jam, green fruit roll, cashews, chocolate chips; 6. Maria "sweetly" tricked her friends on April Fools' Day. 7. vanilla ice cream, marshmallow fluff, yellow pudding; 8. black olives, green peppers, mushrooms

Pages 22–23

1. hard worker, brave, fast-thinking, quick-acting; 2. scared, helpless, sick, alarmed; 3. Answers will vary. 4. Both: good students; Lindsay: persistent, courageous; Erica: frightened, grateful, appreciative; 5. Henry Heimlich; 6. Mount Waialeale; 7. just under 2"; 8. Answers will vary.

Pages 24–25

1. positive: He sees his friend, Eric., He learns Home Run Harvey is the coach.; negative: He could not play baseball with his friends., He sees a player on his new team strike out. 2. He would not get to see his friends and have Coach Dave whom he loved. 3. when he saw Eric; 4. Answers will vary. 5. excited, remorseful; 6. What Juan thought was going to be a negative experience soon looked like it could be a positive one. 7. Answers will vary.

Pages 26–27

1. Tuesday and Wednesday; 2. Monday; 3. Answers will vary. Suggested answers: go to the movies, go to the mall, go bowling, go to a museum, go to the library; 4. Wednesday, Thursday, Friday; 5. Answers will vary. Possible answer: They are probably not pleased. They want to do all kinds of outdoor activities, and it is going to be cold and rainy. 6. no clouds with a high of 82; It is the best forecast for doing outside activities. 7. lingering; 8. athletic, energetic; 9. goggles, sunglasses, cooler with

drinks, sunscreen; 10. Paragraphs will vary.

Pages 28–29

main characters: the colonists; setting: east coast of America; problem: The colonists wanted their independence from Britain. solution: Delegates met to try to help gain independence from Britain. When their efforts did not work, they agreed to go to war.

			i	m	p	o	s	e	d				d	
s		b						e					e	
o		r						r			f		l	
l		a		i	m	m	i	g	r	a	t	e	e	
d		v						a			i		g	
i	n	d	e	p	e	n	d	e	n	c	e		a	
e				r				n			t		t	
r				o				t			i		e	
s				s							o		s	
				p							n			
				e										
				r										

Pages 30–31

1. B, C, A; 2. a. E, C; b. C, E; c. E, C; d. E, C; 3. Since it was a beautiful day, Janie and Jake's mom was taking them to the beach. 4. Janie: because Hayley had recently had Janie over to play; Jake: because he and Charlie went everywhere together; 5. Answers will vary.

Page 32

1. Pluto; 2. Jupiter; 3. Uranus; 4. Neptune; 5. Earth; 6. Saturn; 7. Mercury; 8. Mars; 9. Venus

Page 33

Grant: Washington; Spencer: Arizona; Kara: Pennsylvania; Jack: Massachusetts; All live in Maine.

Pages 34–35

1. to run errands and shop; 2. Answers will vary.

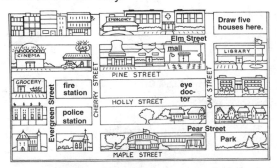

Pages 36–37

Chart: Dairy—milk, yogurt, ice cream, cheese, milkshake; Vegetables—carrots, peas, corn, broccoli, cauliflower; Grains—oatmeal, wheat bread, rice, crackers, pasta; Fruits—banana, apple, grapes, strawberries, pear; Meat & Fish—chicken nuggets, ham, hamburger, fish sticks, pork chops; Fats/Sweets—chocolate chip cookies, candy bar, doughnuts, chocolate cake, cheesecake; 1. She eats right and exercises. 2. hamburger, chicken, ribs; 3. Answers will vary. 4. E, C; 5. Katie: banana, oatmeal; Jimmy: candy bar, ham, corn; Toni: chocolate chip cookies, chicken nuggets, carrots; Anna: fish sticks, pear

Page 38

1. spring; 2. Mother's Day; 3. because they are having a sale; 4. Answers will vary. Possible answer: It was spring. Many people shop for plants in the spring, so a sale would not be needed. 5. because they are buy one get one free; 6. because the sale ends Tuesday

Page 39

1. They love it. 2. They are sad., They do not they will do without their good friends. 3. They think it sounds like a fun, interesting part of the country. 4.

Pages 40–41

1. Most whales are enormous creatures. 2. Whales might look a lot like fish, but the two are very different. 3. Whales can be divided into two groups—baleen and toothed. 4. Blubber is very important to whales and has many purposes. 5. Most whales are enormous creatures. Whales might look a lot like fish, but the two are very different. Whales can be divided into two groups—baleen and toothed. Blubber is very important to whales and has many purposes. 6. Whale: can hold breath for long time, tail fin sideways, lungs; Fish: gills, live in ponds, tail fin up and down; Both: live in oceans, people love to watch

Pages 42–43

1. O, O, F, O, F, F, F, O; 2. Answers will vary. 3. Answers will vary. 4. brave, strong, daring, athletic; 5. climbing poles, ice axes, breathing masks; 6. Answers will vary. 7. Answers will vary.

Pages 44–45

1. to entertain; 2. Working is not what the author would choose to do. 3. The author wants to escape from worries and be free like animals. 4. worries, chores, homework; 5. bird: fly, float, sing, play, soar; dolphin: splash, play, dive, flip; bear: jump, climb, sleep, run, play, fish; dog: play ball, jump, run, roll over, fetch, rest, catch; 6. F, O, F, F, O

Page 46

1. to persuade; 2. Answers will vary. 3. Answers will vary. Possible reasons: Students would get around more quickly., Students would learn more., It would lead to better health. 4. Answers will vary.